T0078436

Healing
THE Broken
PIECES

COPING WITH
PREGNANCY LOSS

Heather S. Cox, RN, BSN

WESTBOW
PRESS®
A DIVISION OF THOMAS NELSON
& ZONDERVAN

This book is a work of non-fiction. Unless otherwise noted, the author and the publisher make no explicit guarantees as to the accuracy of the information contained in this book and in some cases, names of people and places have been altered to protect their privacy.

WestBow Press books may be ordered through booksellers or by contacting:

WestBow Press
A Division of Thomas Nelson & Zondervan
1663 Liberty Drive
Bloomington, IN 47403
www.westbowpress.com
844-714-3454

Interior Image Credit: Ronnie Gibbs II

Scripture quotations taken from The Holy Bible, New International Version® NIV® Copyright © 1973 1978 1984 2011 by Biblica, Inc. TM. Used by permission. All rights reserved worldwide.

ISBN: 978-1-6642-1469-9 (sc)
ISBN: 978-1-6642-1468-2 (hc)
ISBN: 978-1-6642-1470-5 (e)

Library of Congress Control Number: 2020923664

Print information available on the last page.

WestBow Press rev. date: 12/9/2020

DEDICATION

To all women who have experienced pregnancy loss or losses. You are strong and brave. You are mothers.

To my four babies in heaven and in my heart, Jackson, Mercy, Micah and Bailey.

CONTENTS

Acknowledgements

First and foremost I would like to thank God. God led me on my journey of healing and showed me how to turn my pain into something good. He led me to share my story so others could be comforted. God placed special people in my path to help me along my healing journey.

I would also like to thank Eric Schroeder and the WestBow Press team. You encouraged me and helped me to be able to share my story with the world. The WestBow Press team was with me every step of this process. I would like to extend a special thank you to Hanna, Leandra and Kellie. Thank you to all of you for allowing me to turn my dream into a reality.

A special thanks to authors, Kathe Wunnenberg and Heather Gillis. Thank you for your encouragement and feedback during my publishing journey. You are both exceptional authors and wonderful role models to me and all other women.

I would like to thank Ronnie Gibbs II for his encouragement in writing this book. I would also like to thank him for taking the author photos.

I would like to extend a big thank you to the Osborne Baptist Church GriefShare team leaders and members. You are all my family, and I have a special place in my heart for each and every one of you. Thank you for your kindness and encouragement over the last five years. You all are truly a blessing to me. Ronnie Bullins— you are such a great leader. Thank you for your encouragement and feedback with this book. Thank you for helping me grow in my faith with God and showing me the goodness of others. God bless you! Gina— thank you for being there when I needed you and always being such a big support. Andrea— I am so glad our paths crossed and you are in my life. You are a strong woman and I appreciate all of your prayers. Jenny—you have no idea how much you encouraged me the first night I came to Osborne Baptist Church. Thank you for sharing your story. I continued on my journey to healing because of you.

Thank you to my nursing girls. Thank you for being there for me through the years and on hard days. Donna, Cody, and Leslie, you are all so wonderful! Also thank you to Martha, Michelle, Carla Ann, Angie, Amy, Jennifer, Mary and Tara. You all are wonderful women who always offered your support and love. Thank you to all of my nursing staff for your kindness and understanding. Mama Pam, I love you! You have been with me for the last twelve years. You always seem to be there whenever I needed you. You are a blessing in my life!

To my wonderful family, I love you and thank you. Mama and Daddy—thank you for always encouraging me to pursue my dreams. Cox family— I thank you for always supporting me and believing in me. Linda— thanks for being my listening ear and my strength. Aunt Di —thank you for always having my back. Big brother John and my sisters, Stephanie and Ashleigh, thank you for always loving me and being there for me.

To the love of my life, Drew, thank you for always encouraging me, believing in me, and loving me. Thank you for all your help with this book and listening to my ideas for months. Thank you for giving me the courage to share my story. I am so grateful to be sharing my life with you. To my beautiful babies in heaven— Jackson, Mercy, Micah, and Bailey—this book is in honor of you.

Lastly, thank you to strangers and people that have crossed my path along my healing journey. You made an impact on me with your unexpected kindness and understanding.

Thank you to everyone in my healing journey. I am so blessed by the goodness and comfort that came to me.

Introduction
MY STORY

Pregnancy loss is the least acknowledged form of loss. Society does not see it as real or an actual human being that died. Women are made to feel ashamed by their loss and forced to remain silent. A heavy sound of silence surrounds all pregnancy losses. I want to break this silence!

These next pages you will read my story, your story, our story, as women who have suffered an unbearable loss. Whether it is a miscarriage, ectopic pregnancy, or stillborn baby, we have suffered the greatest loss of our lives. I want you to know that every pregnancy loss was a baby, a child, a human being that mattered. You do not have to suffer in silence, hiding your loss in isolation. Through my own journey of multiple pregnancy losses, I have learned the importance of sharing my story.

My story starts many years ago. I experienced three pregnancy losses in just a few years. At the time, I did not fully comprehend the magnitude of these losses. I was in pain but only a few people including my husband knew about them. It was something that I kept buried inside me for many years. Therefore, I think I allowed my emotions towards the losses to be pushed down deep and I became numb.

I had seen firsthand how loss affected families. When I was a baby, my oldest brother had been killed in a car accident. I saw how traumatic it was for my family. So remaining numb seemed to be the answer. Years passed and life happened. My husband and I experienced other losses in our lives. Deaths of friends, uncles, grandparents, and pets had occurred. All of these losses hurt, but they were fully acknowledged by family, friends, and those around us. I would not understand the importance of acknowledgement until later in my journey. As I continued to bury my emotions over my pregnancy losses, they kept trying to resurface. You can only keep things repressed inside for so long until they explode.

An event occurred that stopped me in my tracks. A friend of mine who I had taken dancing lessons with my whole life was shot and killed. She was a reporter and was killed on live television. She was a wonderful person. This event triggered me to remember all other traumatic events in my life. As a result, I began having terrible anxiety and panic attacks. I knew deep down they were caused by unresolved grief. At this point I joined a GriefShare group at a church near my work. I am a registered nurse at a hospital so seeing life and death is a part of my daily job. I have helped many families with dealing with their losses. However, I realized I needed help with my own losses. During my journey through GriefShare class, I found that I had deep pain from my pregnancy losses.

I had suffered alone for so many years. I needed to grieve my babies. The only way was to feel everything—every emotion I had stuffed for years. I ended up suffering a fourth miscarriage during this time period. My journey was not easy and I am still on the road to healing. However, I wanted to share my story to bring comfort to others who have suffered pregnancy losses. It is so important to know you are not alone and you can break your silence by telling the world about your baby or babies. They did exist. In these next chapters I pray that you find comfort, peace, and healing.

God bless you.
Heather

OUT OF THE
SLIMY PIT

I waited patiently for the Lord,
he turned to me and heard my
cry. He lifted me out of the slimy
pit, out of the mud and mire, he
set my feet on a rock and gave
me a firm place to stand.

—Psalms 40:1–3

Denial is something we all use to block out pain. If we bury our losses or pretend they did not happen, then our hearts will not ache. For me, it was easy to live in denial about my pregnancy losses for years because my family and friends never brought them up. I always kept busy to distract myself from feeling or thinking about it. I graduated from nursing school and worked full time as a registered nurse at a local hospital. I remained busy visiting family. I have a large family. I have four siblings and my parents. My husband and I also spent time with his family. We would have dinners with our friends and go on vacations. This seemed to help me keep my pregnancy losses buried for a while. But they were always there. Sometimes my mind would start playing games of "what if," and I would stop those thoughts immediately. When the memories of my body bleeding and those horrific cramps would surface, I would block them out. I did not want to remember my body failing me. The pain was too unbearable. I lived and suffered this way for many years.

> It is absolutely terrifying the kind of deep suffering the happiest looking people are able to hide inside themselves.
> —Nikita Gill

I now know living with this wall of denial was unhealthy and delayed my journey of healing. During these years I had moments of darkness and pain that I hid away. It is so hard to break down the wall of denial. But once it starts breaking down, you can never go back to living in denial—your heart will not let you. During my work as a nurse I took care of patients who had lost pregnancies. I never knew what to say to make them feel better, as I was struggling with my own pain. So I would silently pray for them and their families. Now I wish I had said more and shared my story with them. GriefShare classes helped destroy my denial. As I listened to others talk about the loss of their loved ones, I realized I had experienced loss as well. I could no longer stuff my emotions inside and bury my feelings. My heart and mind could no longer deny the truth. I had lost my babies, my children. It was as if my heart had been numb and frozen, and it was finally starting to melt. After that, all other emotions came.

two
I AM A MOTHER

For you created my inmost being; you knit me together in my
mother's womb.

—Psalms 139:13

Before I formed you in the womb,
I knew you.

—Jeremiah 1:5

What is being said in these Bible
verses? God is saying he created your baby and knew your
child before your child even existed in your
womb. Your baby was always part of God's
plan and is a human being just like you
and me.

My wall of denial was broken down. I
needed to face and feel the truth. I had lost
four babies. I have no living children, but
I am a mother. No matter how many children you have living or in heaven, you are a
mother to each and every one of those babies.

Acknowledgment! Acknowledgment is one of the most important things to me. Once I was able to face and grieve the loss of my babies, I needed others to as well. The members of my GriefShare group were so wonderful in acknowledging my losses and seeing me as a mother. My husband was extremely supportive as well. The world does not always see pregnancy loss that way. Unfortunately, some friends and family did not see pregnancy loss as real loss. To not be acknowledged as a mother and to not have my babies acknowledged as my children was probably the greatest pain I have ever experienced.

I had finally broken down my wall and was feeling so many emotions at once. I needed everyone to acknowledge my babies as I was finally able to.

Miscarriages are labor, miscarriages are birth. To consider

them less dishonors the woman whose womb held life, however briefly.

—Kathryn Miller Ridiman

The world may never notice if a rosebud does not bloom, or even pause to wonder if the petals fall too soon. But every life that ever forms or ever comes to be, touches the world in some small way for all eternity.

—Unknown

I remember how I felt each time I had found out that I was pregnant. I felt excitement, nervousness, joy, and worry—all the emotions that women feel. I felt different. It was as if I already began to bond with my babies in my stomach from the very beginning. I loved them. They were my children. Even though they are in heaven now, they are still my babies. I think about them every day —all four of them. I am and will always be their mother.

> No one else will ever know the strength of my love for you. After all, you are the only one who knows what my heart sounds like from the inside.
>
> —Kristen Proby

The question I hate the most in the world is how many children do you have? It is a common question for most people. However, if you have experienced a pregnancy loss, it is a dreaded question. You ask yourself if you should count the babies you have lost. Do you just simply say none so you do not make the person asking uncomfortable? My suggestion is that you answer in whatever way makes *you* feel the most comfortable. I do not have any living children, so most people just assume my husband and I have no children. It makes me wonder if I count as a mother. Through my journey of healing, God has answered this question for me many times. Yes, I am still a mother. My babies are with him, and I still count as a mother. God tells us through his Word that our wombs held life. I will be the mother to those babies for the rest of my life.

It is very difficult and painful when others do not acknowledge your pregnancy loss. Please remember that you are not alone. God knows your babies, and He is taking care of them. In fact, they still exist and are with God. You did not just have a "pregnancy loss." Your child died. You are their mother. Knowing that God made and acknowledged my babies comforted me when others did not see it that way. God has your babies, and they are safe.

Once you are able to acknowledge your loss, you are often filled with wonder.

I wondered what my child would have looked like. Would my babies look more like me or their father? Would they have my nose? Would my daughter take dance lessons like me? Would my sons play soccer like my husband? What would they grow up to be like? What career choices would they make? Would they get married or have children of their own? A lifetime full of wonder fills our minds after pregnancy loss. I take comfort in knowing I will meet my children in heaven one day and have some questions answered. It is okay to wonder about your babies. Please know that you will find answers when you meet them in heaven. During a particularly sad time in my life, I was praying and asking God to let me know that my babies were okay. I had a dream that night. In that dream I saw God holding my babies in his arms. I was filled with hope and comfort. Pray to God. He will bring you comfort.

three
DIGGING UP
BITTER ROOTS

See to it that no one falls short of the grace of God and that no bitter root grows up to cause trouble and defile many.

—Hebrews 12:15

was now able to acknowledge the loss of my babies. This brought on a whole new set of emotions. I was surprised at how quickly I was able to be angered. Any small or insignificant thing a person said or did seemed to cause me to become angry. I was initially not able to realize why. I was reminded of all those years I had buried my pain and realized that I had buried anger too. Anger is a normal reaction to loss and is a part of grief. From the outside, I seemed fine, but on the inside, I was about to explode. I saw myself and my heart as a garden. The garden had all kinds of beautiful, colorful flowers. The flowers were tall and the garden appeared healthy. However, if you took a closer look you could see deeply rooted weeds and vines with thorns buried under all of the flowers. I needed to pull those weeds and dig up those roots to face my anger. I had lost my babies. Who or what was I angry at? No specific person. I was angry that my sisters and friends could have babies without any trouble. I was angry that mothers on drugs still gave birth to healthy babies. I was angry at my own body. I felt my body had failed me. I felt that it was not fair. Why did my babies have to die? I was mad at a doctor who had told me in an uncaring manner that I was miscarrying my baby. I was angry at family members who acted like it was no big deal. I was angry at other women who were pregnant and had healthy babies. I was just angry. Through my anger, I never blamed God. I was never angry at him. I just did not understand. If you are struggling with being angry with God, it is okay. Talk to him.

Pray to him. He will help you through your anger. You have to dig up those bitter roots and allow yourself to feel anger if needed. Just do not hold onto anger too long, because God can and will turn your anger into peace if you let him. Through my journey, I still have moments of anger or events that trigger me to become angry. One day my husband and I were driving through our neighborhood. As we were driving, we noticed one of the houses had a blue bow on the mailbox. The family that lived there had had a baby boy. I was angry that I could not have had my babies and put bows on my mailbox. Another time, my husband and I were attending church on Mother's Day. They were giving all the mothers roses or corsages to wear. Of course, I did not get one. I was hurt and angry. I wanted to say but I am a mother too! Anger in grief comes in waves, as do many other emotions. One day the waves are slow and calm and the next they are crashing against you. This is all part of the journey. Pray to God to help you release any anger you are holding onto related to your pregnancy loss. He will help you turn it into peace.

> My dear brothers and sisters, take note of this: Everyone should be quick to listen, slow to speak, and slow to become angry, because human anger does not produce the righteousness that God desires.
>
> —James 1: 19—20

WHY?

We do not know why things happen the way they do. We do not understand why our pregnancies ended in loss. It is only natural to want answers, to want to know why. There may be physical reasons why this happened. Through my journey I have seen several doctors. All had different reasons why I was having multiple pregnancy losses. One blamed it on my hormones. One said I had a problem with my cervix. One said there was nothing physically wrong with my body. Through these visits, I still do not have a clear medical answer as why this happened to me. I hope you have some medical answers to understand your loss. The truth is that most women never really get an answer to the why question. A lot of women start to blame themselves. I know I analyzed everything surrounding my pregnancy losses. I wondered if I had been too stressed, or if I did not drink enough water. Maybe I ate something that I should not have. Did I take all my vitamins? Did I get enough sleep? These are questions you may have asked yourself as well. It is easy to start blaming yourself and feeling guilty. You wonder if you did something wrong. You wonder if you somehow caused your loss. But, blaming yourself and feeling guilty is false guilt. False guilt is when you feel bad even though you have done nothing wrong. Be careful not to blame yourself or get stuck in guilt. Pregnancy loss happens and most of the time we do not know why. Turn to God and pray about it. He has a plan for you.

> Jesus replied, you do not realize now what I am doing but later you will understand.
>
> —John 13:7

Maybe you went through it and survived it just so you could help someone else make it through.
—Quote by Awakened Spirit

Your pregnancy loss will always be something you may not understand or wonder about. Unfortunately we do not always get the answers in this life. We sometimes question God as to why things happen. It is hard to accept that we may never get answers. We may wonder what God's plan is for our lives. But we have to learn to trust him and let him guide our lives.

Be still and know that I am God.
—Psalms 46:10

There are so many things that I do not know. I do not know why bad things happen. I do not know why I lost my babies, but I have to believe that God has a plan for me and you. God loves me and you. He is always here for us. I have experienced the bad, and I have experienced darkness in my life. However, God has always shown up. We are never alone. No matter what, we have to put our faith in God. He is with us, even in the darkness.

> In him was life, and that life was the light of all mankind. The light shines in the darkness and the darkness has not overcome it.
>
> —John 1: 4—5

Five
A BROKEN HEART

The Lord is close to the broken-hearted and saves those who are crushed in spirit.

—Psalms 34:18

The journey of pregnancy loss is a marathon, not a sprint. It is an ongoing process that you live with daily. All kinds of emotions can surface at any time. Once your anger dissipates, sadness and depression can hit you hard. It is okay to not be okay. You lost a baby. You lost your child. Your heart is broken. It is okay to be sad. It is okay to have days where all you do is stay home and grieve. You may feel that your pain and sadness is too much to bear. Remember that God is with you. You lost your baby. You lost your baby or child at all of the ages of their life. You are grieving for dreams and a future that will not happen. There have been days and nights during my journey when I felt I could not handle the pain. So I prayed to God. I talked and cried to my husband. I cried on my dog. You are allowed to cry. Let those tears out. I cried so many times but I kept going. Do not give up, but allow yourself permission to grieve, to cry. God hears our cries and sees our pain.

> Tears are prayers too. They travel to God when we can't speak.
> —Psalms 56:8

> Blessed are those who mourn, for they will be comforted.
> —Matthew 5:4

> Jesus wept.
> —John 11:35

It is difficult to handle our sadness sometimes. During my work as a nurse I have taken care of many women who have experienced pregnancy loss. One day, I remember I was rounding on the birthing center unit. A mother had given birth to a stillborn baby boy hours before. I walked into the nursery and saw the beautiful stillborn baby boy wrapped in a blanket laying in a bassinet. All of a sudden I could not swallow. I felt tears filling my eyes. All I could think about was my babies. Physical pain filled my chest as I tried to keep my composure. My heart actually hurt. I felt such sorrow for this baby's mother and also sadness for the loss of my own babies.

Grief can hit us at any moment and can be triggered by large or small things. Sometimes our sorrow feels too heavy. It is easy to get into a depressive state during your time of mourning. Try to go outside, be in nature. Call or talk to a trusting friend or family member. If needed go see a counselor, or join a GriefShare group at your church or another local church. I cannot tell you how much attending GriefShare class helped me. I was able to relate to others who had similar losses. You find other people who have had pregnancy losses along your journey. They become family to you and understand you and your loss more than anyone else could. God places these people in our path to help us through our journey.

The pain of losing my babies is heartache unlike anything else I have ever experienced in my life. I will always miss them and grieve for them. It seems strange to say I miss my babies when I never met them. I miss the future I would have shared with them. They were still a part of me even if they did not stay a long time. It still brings great pain. The pain and sadness does not go away but you learn to live with it. You learn it is okay to have bad days where you are sad. You learn that it is okay to cry. There are events in life that will trigger your sadness and pain. These events will remind you of your loss or losses. You may cry at unexpected and inconvenient moments. It is okay. Do not be too hard on yourself. You need to let that pain go. Cry. Cry to God. He is there.

> A voice is heard in Ramah, mourning and great weeping. Rachel weeping for her children and refusing to be comforted because her children are no more.
> —Jeremiah 31: 15

In the Bible, Rachel is remembered as the mother who mourns for her children. All she wanted was to become a mother. I can relate to Rachel as I have cried for my babies. My heart will never be the same. My life will never be the same as there will always be something missing— my babies. I know God heard Rachel's cries, as he hears yours and mine. He will bring you comfort. I have taken comfort in knowing that my babies are in Heaven with God. They are safe.

> He heals the brokenhearted and bandages their wounds.
>
> —Psalms 147:3

six
THE RIGHT TO GRIEVE

To not have your suffering rec-
ognized is an almost unbearable
form of violence.

—Quote by Andrei Lankov

Please be patient with me. You
see, I lost my child. And while it
might seem like a long time to
you. It is every day for me.

—Quote by Donna Waag

I want to tell you that you have the right
to grieve your pregnancy losses. Family,
friends and the rest of the world may not
understand. For me, this made the pain of
my losses worse. It is extremely hard if you
have announced your pregnancy to others
and then have to tell them that your baby
died. Co-workers avoid you because they
do not know what to say. Some friends and
family are so busy that they do not have
time to reach out to you. Some see it as no

big deal or think it is not a real living human being. No one in my family had ever experienced a miscarriage so they did not and could not understand. Again, acknowledgement is a big part of this. I felt the need for the world to acknowledge my babies and to see my losses as real pain.

> Don't forget that when people lose a baby they aren't just losing a newborn. They are also losing their toddler taking their first step. Their child starting to read. Their teenager graduating high school. Their grown child getting married to the love of their life. They are losing every magical moment. In the blink of an eye, the future was erased.
>
> —Quote by Zoe Clark-Coates

Unfortunately, when a woman experiences a pregnancy loss, whether miscarriage, ectopic pregnancy, or stillborn birth, people do not understand. People say all the wrong things that can be very hurtful and minimize the pain that the mother is going through.

Some examples of comments said to grieving mothers that cause pain are:

1. It was early. It was not a baby yet.
2. You are young. You can try again.
3. At least you weren't further along in your pregnancy.
4. There was obviously something wrong with the baby.
5. This happens to everyone. It is no big deal.
6. You will be fine in a couple of days.
7. At least you did not know your baby.
8. You can just adopt.
9. Everything happens for a reason.

I have had friends and family say some of these things to me. While I understand they may not know what to say, it still hurts. You are already mourning the loss of your baby so these comments can cause even more pain. Try to forgive these people who have hurt you.

> Bless those who curse you, pray
> for those who mistreat you.
> > —Luke 6:28

> The words of the reckless pierce
> like swords, but the tongue of
> the wise brings healing.
> > —Proverbs 12:18

During your time of grief over your loss, try to surround yourself with those who are supportive. These people may be church friends, members from your GriefShare class, supportive family members or your spouse. It is also okay to spend some time alone or time alone with your spouse. Try to ignore any hurtful comments from those who do not understand. It is hard to ignore but, learning to ignore teaches us grace. In time, try to forgive those people for hurting you. Throughout your journey, keep in mind that you have the right to grieve. Take as much time as you need. Remember that God sees your pain even if others do not. He is on this journey with you.

seven

DADS HURT TOO

God so loved the world that He gave His one and only son, that whosoever believes in him shall not perish but have everlasting life.

—John 3:16

I will never forget the look on my husband's face when I told him I was miscarrying one of our babies. I will never forget the sound of his voice on the phone when I told him about another baby that I was miscarrying. Fathers of pregnancy loss are often forgotten about. I cannot imagine how hard it is to be the man feeling helpless and watching your wife grieve. Men grieve too. All of their dreams of the future with their baby or child are destroyed. They are made to think they have to stay strong and show no emotions. The truth is that fathers have lost their baby or babies too. I talked with my husband to further understand the father's perspective of pregnancy loss.

His initial feeling with our first two miscarriages was shock. He did not think of pregnancy loss as even being a possibility. He also stated that he did not know how to feel or what to do. He was basically lost. He could not believe that our babies were gone. However, with our fourth pregnancy loss, he felt immediate sadness. He was hopeful that everything would work out. During this time my husband said he never really felt anger. He did feel as though he could talk with me about our losses and share his feelings. Additionally, he said he talked with his parents about it. My husband said he felt confused and did not understand why this happened to us. He wanted answers.

Mothers and fathers handle loss differently. Women may feel they can show their emotions, while men may hide theirs. Some men get angry and some do not. Loss can also bring couples together. Mothers and fathers can relate to each other's feelings of loss. They can feel sad together. They can talk about what their baby or babies would have looked like or acted like. They can comfort each other and discuss their feelings.

As you travel through your journey of pregnancy loss, remember that Dads hurt too. They may not always show it, but they lost their child too. All their dreams of the future with their child are completely lost and erased so quickly. It may help your husband or significant other to talk to their father or close friend about their feelings. I know that my husband is more comfortable talking to a family member or friend one on one. Sometimes it is easier for fathers to express emotions about their loss in private. Encourage them to talk about it and support them. Remind them that they are still fathers to the babies they have lost. Fathers need acknowledgement too.

eight
ONE STEP FORWARD, TWO STEPS BACK

The journey through pregnancy loss is like a roller coaster ride. You will have ups and downs. You will feel denial, anger, sadness, and joy at times. It is a long road filled with unexpected emotions. Sometimes during my journey I would feel anger. I would also feel sadness and loneliness. There were times that I felt healing. I would think I was doing better and then I would be triggered by different things. Waves of grief or anger may come out of nowhere. Do not let this discourage you. Triggers are going to happen to you. I still cannot walk down the baby aisle of the grocery store without feeling sad. I see women pushing strollers with babies at the park, and I feel heartache all of a sudden. When I would see a pregnant woman I would feel envious. One of my miscarriages occurred while I was working at the hospital. I actually passed my baby in one of the bathrooms. For months after this I could not go into that bathroom. It reminded me of the pain and sadness of that terrible day. Life is full of triggers and they are everywhere. You have to learn to let your feelings come and let them pass. It is okay to feel better one day and then feel sad the next. This does not mean you are not healing, and it does not mean you will feel this way forever. As we learn in the Bible, there is a time for everything in life.

> There is a time for everything and a season for every activity under the heavens, a time to be born, a time to die, a time to plant and a time to uproot, a time to kill and a time to heal, a time to tear down and a time to build, a time to weep and a time to laugh, a time to mourn, and a time to dance. A time

to scatter stones and a time to gather them, a time to embrace and a time to refrain, a time to search and a time to give up, a time to keep and a time to throw away, a time to tear and a time to mend, a time to be silent, a time to speak, a time to love and a time to hate, a time for war and a time for peace.

—Ecclesiastes 3: 1—8

There is a time for everything in life. God has a plan for us and knows what is best for us. Your sadness will not last forever. God will help you heal. Along my journey I have experienced many setbacks to healing. I felt as though I would never feel better. God knows your heart and sees your suffering. Turn to him and he will allow you to feel joy again.

He will yet fill your mouth
with laughter and your lips with
shouts of joy.

—Job 8:21

The important thing to remember on
your journey is to always keep trying.
Reach out to God or supportive family
or friends when you feel disappointment
or discouragement. Attending GriefShare
class helped me in times that I felt discour-
aged. God puts people in our paths to help
us during these times.

We're stronger in places that
we've been broken.
—Quote by Ernest Hemingway

You are stronger than you think. You
will find strength in yourself that you
never knew was there. As you heal, God
will put people in your life that are on a
similar journey as you. You will find that

sharing your story and helping them, helps you heal as well. As a nurse, I have seen many women who have experienced pregnancy loss. Although this triggers my own emotions to surface, it also allows me to be there for them. I take care of them and let them know I understand their pain and know that their babies were real.

The loss of my babies has taught me to be patient with myself. I will start feeling better and then have moments of pain or missing my children. After my miscarriages, I remember my stomach feeling empty. I felt empty. I missed my baby being inside me. I remember touching my abdomen and feeling lost. The journey of pregnancy loss will last throughout my life. However, God has a plan for me and for you. He will not let us stop healing.

He who began a good work in
you will carry it on to completion.
—Philippians 1:6

nine
LET IT GO

You may be wondering what I mean when I say let it go. I am not talking about your baby or their memory. Through my journey of loss, there are many times I have had to learn to let things go. First of all, you may need to let people go from your life. Unfortunately, some people are too uncomfortable with your loss and cannot handle it. They may avoid you altogether or they may never mention or acknowledge your loss. These people may have avoided you during the initial stages of your loss. They may not understand why you are "not acting like yourself" or why you cannot "get over it". Friends or family that behave this way are not supportive and do not contribute to your healing. These are the people in your life that you may have to let go.

I have also learned that after you experience pregnancy loss, your perspective changes. Small things that seemed to matter no longer cross your mind with worry. You avoid insignificant conflict going on between others in your life. These things no longer exist on your list of worries or cares. Certain expectations that are placed on you by family, friends, or work do not matter. You do not have to care. You learn to take care of yourself, and you learn to say no. These are all examples of things that you let go of.

It is important to try to let go of bitterness or anger you feel towards others related to your loss. You may still feel hurt by comments made to you about your pregnancy loss. You may be disappointed in your family or friends who you felt were not there for you during this time. Also, you may be upset with medical personnel and how your pregnancy loss was handled or explained. You need to try and allow these feelings to pass. Let them go. Holding on to these hurts will only hinder your healing. You need to talk and pray to God. Ask him to help you let go. Letting go of these hurts is not easy. It is something you have to work on and pray about on an ongoing basis. Time does help but also making the decision to let your hurts go leads to healing.

> Therefore if any man be in Christ, he is a new creature: old things are passed away; behold, all things are becoming new.
> —2 Corinthians 5:17

> Trust in the Lord with all your heart and lean not on you own understanding.
> —Proverbs 3:5

> At all times we must learn to forget the past and forge ahead. If we fail to let go of the past, it is very difficult to move forward.
> —Isaiah 43: 18—19

ten

THE HEALING HAS BEGUN

I have heard your prayers, and
seen your tears, I will heal you.
—2 Kings 20:5

God sees our grief and he wants to help us heal. I experienced a great amount of healing when I realized my babies were with God. I knew they were safe in Heaven and that God was taking care of them. My babies never had to experience the pain and suffering of this earthly world. They went straight from my womb into Heaven. It brought me great comfort to imagine God holding my babies in his lap. God has your babies too. Babies that died in our wombs were born straight into the glory of Heaven. We will see them again one day. Realizing this brought me healing and comfort. I hope it helps you as well.

Our babies are dancing on streets
of gold within those pearly gates.
—Revelation 21:21

While I am still on my journey to healing, I have discovered ways to bring comfort to myself and to others. I have found
that sharing my story with others helps me.
I encourage you to share your story when
you are ready. Talking to other women that
have experienced pregnancy loss will help
you and them. These women will become
an important part of your life. They understand how you feel when others simply cannot. When you reach out and help others,
you are healing as well. I have experienced
this firsthand. I have met other women at
church, at work, or through acquaintances
that have experienced pregnancy loss.
Sharing our stories with each other is extremely therapeutic. I felt joy from sharing
and relating to these women. Sharing heals

broken pieces in our hearts. God wants us to comfort others as he has comforted us.

> Praise be to the God, the father of compassion and the God of all comfort, who comforts us in all our troubles, so that we can comfort those in any trouble with the comfort we ourselves receive from God.
> —2 Corinthians 1: 3—4

> Two are better than one, because they have a good return for their labor. If either of them falls down, one can help the other up.
> —Ecclesiastes 4: 9—10

When you experience pregnancy loss or any loss for that matter, you learn to experience joy and sadness together. It seems odd but these feelings can happen simultaneously. Every day I feel joy and sadness. I am sad that I lost my babies. I am sad missing the loss of the life and future I would have shared with them. However, I also feel joy knowing they are at peace and safe with God in Heaven.

So how do we heal? How do we keep surviving in the midst of our loss? I have found that talking to God, praying, and reading the bible is helpful. There are also many books about pregnancy and infant loss that are wonderful. One book that especially helped me was "Grieving the child I never knew" by Kathe Wunnenberg. Additionally, finding and befriending other women with similar losses is extremely comforting. Also, spending time with supportive family members and friends is therapeutic. My work as a nurse helps me focus on helping others through their pain. Sometimes focusing on helping others allows us to stop being so hurt in our own pain. I know that

I will carry the pain of my losses with me, but I also know that I can survive.

As I continue my journey of healing, I accept that I will have triggers and waves of emotion along the way. I take comfort in knowing God is on my journey with me. He is with you on your journey as well. Therefore, take comfort in knowing he is there. I heard a song during my journey that has touched me. I would like to share some of the lyrics with you. The song is "The Healing has Begun" by Matthew West.

> "There's a world full of people dying from broken hearts, so don't be afraid to show them your beautiful scars, cause they're the proof, you're the proof, the healing has begun."

eleven

THE POWER
OF SONG

Music has always been a big part of my life. Ever since I was younger, I remember seeing my parents dancing to music in the kitchen. My sisters and I would argue over radio stations in the car riding with my parents. When I was celebrating life I would listen to happy, upbeat music. When I was upset or lonely, I would listen to softer, sad songs. I never realized the power that music has on our minds, hearts, and souls. It can bring such joy or sorrow to you. It can make you cry or it can make you smile. Certain songs can take you back in time and bring back past memories. As much as I enjoy the music, I also love reading the lyrics of songs. They speak to us and fill us with different emotions. Music and song can heal our hearts. Through the loss of my babies, I have discovered several songs that have comforted me. Listening to the music and their lyrics fills my whole body with peace.

The following lists of songs are some that I hold dear to my heart:

- "I will carry you" by Selah
- "Small Bump" by Ed Sheeran
- "Amy's Song" by Jonathan David Helser
- "Glory Baby" by Watermark
- "Held" by Natalie Grant
- "Thy Will" by Hilary Scott
- "I still Believe" by Jeremy Camp
- "Through the Fire" by the Crabb family
- "Apron Strings" by Everything but the Girl
- "Blessings" by Laura Story

I hope these songs or any other songs that you find on your journey will bring you comfort. There were so many days and nights that I listened to music when I was hurting from the loss of my babies. The music always soothed me, even if only to allow me to cry and release my pain. I encourage you to allow music to help you heal. I pray that you will be comforted the way that I was. Please search for more songs and music on your journey. There is so much music that has healing power. God has spoken to me so many times through song. All you have to do is listen. God has used music to allow me to grieve and heal.

"Amazing grace, how sweet the sound, that saved a wretch like me. I once was lost but now I am found, was blind and now I see."
—Song by John Newton

twelve
ALWAYS IN OUR HEARTS

Our babies that we have lost are always in our hearts. They stay with us the rest of our lives. There are many ways to honor or memorialize your baby. Mothers who have experienced a stillborn birth can have a funeral or memorial to grieve their child. They may bury their child and have a grave to go visit. This will help them memorialize their baby. On the other hand, mothers who experienced miscarriages, ectopic pregnancies, or other pregnancy losses do not have a baby to bury. Fortunately, there are other ways for them to honor and acknowledge their baby.

For example, you can plant a tree to honor the memory of your baby. This will help you have something to watch grow and remind you that your baby was real and is now in Heaven. Also, many companies will personalize Christmas ornaments for you to honor your baby. My husband and I hang up small stockings from our fireplace every Christmas to honor our babies that have passed away. This comforts me because I feel they are still with us celebrating Christmas, if only in our hearts.

The United States of America acknowledges pregnancy loss. Our country honors Pregnancy and Infant Loss Awareness on October fifteenth of every year. You can wear a ribbon or light a candle on that day to honor your lost babies. Some cities even have special walks to remember the babies that you have lost and many other events you can participate in.

You can also write a letter to your baby or babies. I have personally written letters to all of my babies that I have lost. It is just something personal between you and your child. Writing these letters has helped me to release my thoughts and opened up my heart to healing.

Additionally, some women say that releasing balloons in their babies' memory is comforting. You can write your child's name on the balloon and release it into the sky. Many times I have bought Happy Birthday balloons. I release them into the sky on my babies' would be due dates. I used to watch the balloon go up into the sky until I could no longer see it. This made me feel closer to my babies.

Tattoos are also a way to honor or memorialize your baby or babies. You can get your babies' name or the date you lost them tattooed on your body. Some women get roses, angel wings, or baby footprints. Men who have lost babies can get a tattoo of a meaningful Bible verse to honor them. There are many tattoo ideas to honor your loss. Tattoos can help parents of child loss feel they can memorialize their children for life.

Another example is jewelry. Jewelry has been one of the most healing items for me. I have several pieces of jewelry honoring my lost babies. I have a necklace shaped as a heart with tiny baby footprints on it. I also have a necklace with four circles on it. Each circle has the name of one of my babies on it. My husband gave me a beautiful necklace one year after we had lost two babies. It had a large silver tree on the front and it said forever family. The back of the necklace was engraved with mine and my husband's name on it, as well as the names of our two babies. Many companies will personalize jewelry of your choice. You can get necklaces, bracelets, or rings to honor your lost babies. My husband and I have matching silicone bracelets. They are plain on the outside and the inside has our last name with the names of our babies imprinted on it. These pieces of jewelry help me to honor my babies. They bring me comfort.

One thing that I recommend as a wonderful healing idea is to name your baby or babies. Your babies that died were real human beings. You can name them to help acknowledge them. This helped me greatly. It made my babies real to me. My husband and I did not name the first two babies that we lost until years later. It does not matter how long it has been. Naming your baby is very healing. I had a feeling with each of my pregnancies whether they were boys or girls. If you are not sure you can use gender neutral names. The names of my four babies are Jackson, Mercy, Micah, and Bailey. I know what age each of them would be now. Most mothers, who have experienced pregnancy loss, always know what age their baby would be.

Before I was born the Lord called me; from my mother's womb, he has spoken my name.

—Isaiah 49:1

In conclusion, no matter how you choose to honor your pregnancy loss, it will bring you comfort. It is a part of our journey that promotes healing and acknowledgement.

Conclusion

Pregnancy loss is real. Every woman who has carried a baby no matter how long is a mother. I am a mother to my four babies. You are a mother to your baby or babies too. Remember acknowledgement is powerful in healing. Naming my babies really helped me to see them as actual people— my children. I encourage you to name your babies. Also, any emotion you feel is okay. It is important to feel them all. Be kind and gentle to yourself. Take time to rest, to grieve, and reach out to others when you need to. My pregnancy loss journey led me into a place of deep pain and darkness at times. Even in that darkness, God filled my life with people placed in my path to be there for me. When I was at work and miscarried one of my babies, my work mother (as I call her) was working. I immediately collapsed in her arms and she took care of me. God ensured she was there with me that day. Another time

I was having a hard time at work with my grief and one of the birthing center nurses was close by. She just hugged me already knowing that I was hurting and why.

A simple smile or hug, or someone acknowledging your pain with a short text message or phone call, are all blessings. They are sent our way by God. Do not fail to recognize these blessings. They heal our broken pieces. God filled my heart with the goodness and kindness of others. There was someone there, and when there wasn't God was always with me. Your pregnancy loss is an ongoing, lifetime journey. God is on the journey with you. Pray and talk to him. He will never leave you.

We have to break the silence of pregnancy loss. We are mothers. We are mothers to babies gone too soon. We are walking around with broken hearts and pieces of those hearts are in Heaven— our babies. A part of us goes with them. We carry the rest of our broken pieces around with us. If you look around, there are mothers like us all around you. We are still living in spite of it all. We will always grieve for our babies. However, God shows us we can heal our broken pieces. I grieve for Jackson, Mercy, Micah and Bailey. They are the four broken pieces of my heart. Through my healing, I like to think that God filled those broken pieces. He filled them with comfort, faith, peace and hope. I pray you feel these throughout your journey as well. God can heal. I am here to tell you that you can and will survive. God has a plan for us, for our future. Remember to keep looking up and have faith in God. There is always hope.

> God can restore what is broken and change it into something amazing, all you need is faith.
> —Joel 2:25

REFERENCES

"Awakened Spirit". Pinterest. 19 February 2019. Web. 10 September 2020. www.pinterest.com.

Clark-Coates, Zoe. "Saying Goodbye". Saying Goodbye. 2017. Web. 9 September 2020. www.sayinggoodbye.org.

"For the Love of Angels". I Am a Mother To An Angel. 9 August 2013. Web. 8 September 2020. www.fortheloveofangels.blogspot.com.

Gill, Nikita. "For You Who Is Suffering In Silence". MindJournal. 8 June 2018. Web. 10 September 2020. www.themindjournal.com.

Hemingway, Ernest. "A Farewell to Arms". PGSG. 15 November 2018. Web. 9 September 2020. www.medium.com.

Lankov, Andrei. Quote Fancy. 2020. Web. 8 September 2020. www.quotefancy.com.

Proby, Kristen. "Fight With Me". (With Me in Seattle, #2). 31 December 2012. Web. 13 November 2020. http://www.goodreads.com/book.

Ridiman, Kathryn Miller. "Angel Baby". Talk Birth. Web. 8 September 2020. www.talkbirth.me.com.

The Holy Bible, New International Version. Zondervan, 1985, 1995, 2002.

Waag, Donna. "Healing While Grieving". YouTube. 6 May 2020. Web. 9 September 2020. www.m.youtube.com.

ABOUT THE AUTHOR

Heather S. Cox has suf-
fered four pregnancy
losses. She finds heal-
ing in sharing her story
with others. Also, she
hopes to bring com-
fort to others who
have experienced sim-
ilar losses. Heather

is a registered nurse who has been prac-
ticing for twelve years. She holds a multi-
state registered nursing license. She has a
Bachelor's degree in Science of Nursing. In
her spare time, she enjoys Pilates, yoga, and
sitting on her front porch. Heather lives

in North Carolina with her husband and dog, Carolina. She enjoys helping others and hopes her story will touch and encourage them.

Printed in the United States
By Bookmasters